Broken But Still Beautiful

Illuminate

Broken But Still Beautiful - Illuminate

ISBN: 9798646879302

First edition: June 2020
Published by h.dcosta

This is a work of creative nonfiction. Some parts have been fictionalized in varying degrees, for various purposes.

For the love that made this possible and the support that made me fall in love with this chaotic madness.

I believe breaking my heart made me realise that I need to love myself more than I love others that walk past my life.

I was hurting and breaking into a million pieces. The darkness was creeping in. These demons kept coming closer.

Then I saw a ray of light, stretched my arms towards it. And at that very moment, you pulled me up. You got me out of the darkness into a brighter place.

The universe sent you to be my light. It put you in places to reach my heart.

At that very moment, the universe only existed to bring us closer. At that very moment, you became my light.

I want nothing much, but to be loved like never before. I want to be kissed when it's dark, and all we can see is the moon and the stars. I want to be hugged and feel like home in your arms. I want to dance In the rain and fall a bit more for you. Not just fall, but pour down like the rain In love with you. I want to live in those eyes, where I see the universe, and at the centre of it, you and me. I want to love you and be loved a bit too. All I want is you to love me today, and then a bit more tomorrow.

I wanted nothing to do with love. But then I looked into your eyes and couldn't help but fall. I tried to resist the urge, but then you smiled. I tried to resist, but then we kissed, and I lost myself. I wanted nothing to do with love. I just wanted to be happy.

These butterflies in my stomach are not excited about love. They're just glad to be accepted.

10

Look how beautiful these scars are.
Look how they tell you stories that
made my heart stronger.

You deserve to be loved more than you think, more than you settle for. You deserve love and every single piece of happiness that comes with it.

Yes, you deserve someone to love you with every heartbeat, till their last breath.

- You deserve LOVE.

12

I have been breaking
I have been falling and hurting
I have been drowning

In this sea of pain
You pushed me into

And you care about me now
When I have already let myself drown

I'm free. No love lost, no pain to gain. I'm free, for I'm breathing fresh air and I have me.

The past, I'm not going to run from it.
It doesn't break me anymore.
It doesn't make me feel low.

The past, it has made my heart stronger.
Stronger than it could ever be.

It can love and yet not be scared of
falling anymore.
It can love and yet not be scared of the
past repeating.

Yes, the past can hurt.
But I have only learned from it.
Never ran from it.
Just made it my strength.
And moved on from it.

You let go because they
are not ready to trust you.
You let go because they
are not ready to love you.
You let go because they
are not ready to hold you.
You let go because deep
down they don't care.

You let go of what means
the world to you.

- Letting go

16

Being loved is rare, and if you are
being loved, don't you throw it away.

It's been hard to sleep. It's been hard to wake up. It's been like that since you left. It's been a strange ride, 'cause I haven't felt anything like that.

You're fire, and I'm ice.
I can't come any closer,
even if I want to.

You're fire, and I'm ice.
Can't you see I'm in love,
and ready to die.

You can't match the amount of love
I have for you in my chest

But you can love me
In some way
In your own ways
In little bits and pieces
In little crumbs

Yes you can love me
A little bit every day
A lot somedays

Keep me closer,
show me hope,
fix me up,
love me the most.

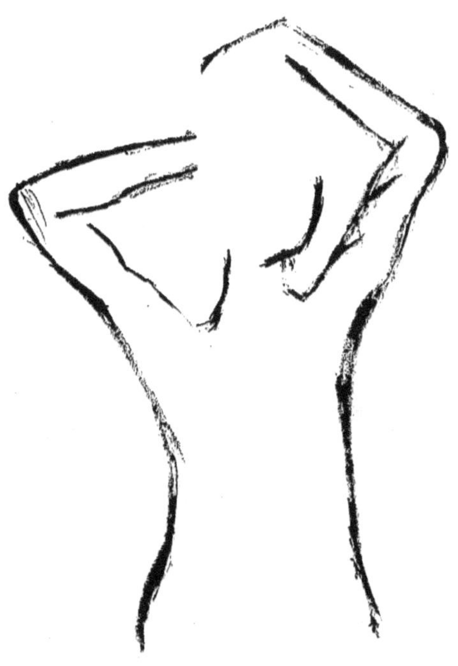

Oh! The way you make me feel. It's like, I can feel every drop of blood run inside. Like a king, I can conquer the world with you besides.

Oh! The way you make me feel. Like life is worth living. Like I want to fall in love, and keep falling.

- The way you make me feel.

None of us are perfect, and if you are here to find the perfect one, good luck. You ain't finding someone like that. We all come with flaws, and that's the beauty of it.

Life itself is a flaw, and if you don't see the beauty in that, then I don't know what you're looking for.

Life is pain, struggle, and so many other things, it's beautiful, and if you have someone to hold your hands through all of it, trust me you are lucky, most people out there don't have this luxury.

So life itself is not perfect. You don't need to be perfect either.

Love your flaws, love yourself, and be you.

With a broken heart,

I will find a way to keep living.
I will find a way to keep healing.
I will find a way to keep loving.

Even with a broken heart,
I will always find a way to keep feeling.

24

Stay away from the ones who ask you to love them and don't love you back in return.

- They are the toxic ones.

You will have my love
when you learn how to
accept me the way I'm.

My heart, this thing is
on fire since you left.

But i don't understand
how it still finds
a way to fall in love?

It's burning,
but falling in love.

It's hurting,
but falling in love.

It's breaking,
but still falling in love.

And i still wonder,
how does my heart still,
find a way to love?

27

You left me all alone in this darkness,
but I found a light, I found myself.

Not everyone you love is going
to love you back, and it's okay.

- Reality Check

Loving you wasn't a mistake.
Believing that you loved me
was a mistake.

If they leave. Just fuck it and move on. They don't deserve you to be holding on to them.

Know that your heart is stronger than you think it is. The more scars, the more pieces, the more pain, the stronger it gets.

It was you that made every drop of blood in me fall in love. It was you that turned those same drops of blood into sadness.

We fall in love

We break in love

We get stronger in love

What's the point of these cracks
if I let them hurt me instead of
making me stronger?

Your heart, it's a beautiful mess, it's not like the rest. Your heart, it's precious. I have seen it fall, I have seen it crave for love. I have seen it give love and bear the pain of not being loved in return. Your heart, I have not seen anything as strong as your heart.

The universe took away all
my lovers and taught me
how to love myself with the
same passion I loved them.

If you're come back to find love for you in my heart, there is plenty of it, but none to give you.

It was time that thought me. My heart can be fixed but can never be the same.

Walk away from the ones who don't love you back. Walk away, because your heart is not meant to be left unloved like that. Your heart is meant to be loved and cherished for the beauty it is. Your heart deserves to be loved in return.

Never let the same person hurt you twice, no matter what they mean to you.

With love, you killed the faith
I had in my heart for love.

Genuine love always finds
a way to love again.

43

A heart filled with love regardless of the pain it's going through is one of the bravest hearts out in the world right now.

- A heart the world needs right now.

I'm tired of fighting for people to stay in my life. If they wanted to stay, I wouldn't have to fight for them to stay in the first place.

I might be lost for now,
but my heart seems to
be in the right place.

We had this dream. We would travel the world hand in hand and make love in different parts of the world. We had a future set in place. But life doesn't seem to be wanting all the things that we dream of doing. Life had a different plan for us. Maybe this is how it's supposed to be. Perhaps we were meant to be in love so that our hearts could hurt and become as strong as it is today. Maybe we were meant to meet lovely souls, but not have them for ourselves the entire time. Perhaps that's what life is trying to teach us. That nothing is here to stay. Things are supposed to break. People are supposed to leave, and hearts are supposed to become stronger. Life may not give us what we desire, but it sure has better plans for us.

We are warriors
We rise from pain
The very pain caused
By the people we love

We are warriors
We rise from pain
The very pain
That broke us
Into million pieces

We are warriors
We rise from pain
And we are the
Strongest of all

We are warriors
We are pain
We are the pieces
They left in vain

I hope you fall in love with someone who loves every piece of you, even on your darkest days.

Love is hard. It demands attention. It requires work. It requires two people to work things out for love to exist.

Love will show you the bad, the good, and every fine detail in between.

Constantly recognize the good, work at the bad parts, and fall in love with the fine details in between.

Because love is not easy, but if you work hard enough, you will be fine.

Love is all that we have. And I will always desire love.

Sometimes even the largest amount of love in your heart can't stop you from losing them. And that's a hard pill to swallow. Not everyone you love will understand the love you have for them in your heart.

I have been down, down for a long time now. And it's hard, but it's time to stand up and be strong. I have done this, and I will do it again. I will stand up, and the day I do, trust me, with the pain, I will dust you off too. I will come back stronger than ever. I will come back changed, with a shield and a dagger. This heart is mine, and I gave it to enough of you to ruin it. This heart is mine, and it's time I protect it. The beginning and the end of another me. It's time, time to close all those broken and open chapters. It's time to burn down the whole book.

- It's time for a change.

Am I ever going to be enough?
Am I ever going to be the one
you always wanted?

I come with flaws,
with broken pieces.
I have never been perfect.
And I never will be.

Will I ever be enough
for you to love me?
Will I ever be enough for you
to keep me just the way I'm?

I was diamond, but you kept chasing for silver.

Look at how they treated your heart, like a soaked sponge, squeezing all the love out of it.

55

Honey was dripping through
every crack in my heart, but
you only noticed the cracks.

Heal, and the battle between
your heart and brain will end.

I don't want to be fixed.
I just want someone to
hold my hand and stay.

And I hope the love I have
for myself is enough to save
me from all my demons.

I hope one day you find someone
who never gives up on you.

Never be sorry for loving too much.
Never be sorry for caring too much.
Never be sorry for being you.

I don't have the time and energy
to be upset or angry with the
ones who don't love me.

- You don't love me, okay bye.

The love you take for granted
today will be stronger tomorrow.
But it won't be yours to keep.

My generation is filled with false lovers, coated in beautiful paint, but damaged inside.

You came into my life like the sun shining bright. But days past and you just turned dark, darker than the empty void of space.

Yes, we all come flawed. It's not new. But the question here is, would you judge me for my flaws, or would you love me for who I'm?

3:09 in the morning and
all I can think of is you and
how you hurt my heart.

You deserve much more than the fake love they promised to give you.

I'm my own lover.

Don't waste your time fighting
back the ones that hurt you.

You are not your past.
You are not your
broken relationships.
You are bigger and better
than those petty things.

71

Don't be foolish to let a cheater
hurt your heart once again.

- True colours never wash away.

72

They hurt you in the name of love. But the truth is, they never knew how to love you.

I wrote about you in books
and burned them all.

You couldn't stop me from falling in love just like I couldn't stop you from leaving.

It's hard to pretend that you don't love them anymore when a part of your heart is not ready to give up.

If you feel love, you feel love.
There is no hiding it or from it.

She had a heart of gold but always gave it to the ones who never treated it like one.

Stop waiting for someone to love you. It's time you start loving yourself for who you are.

Imagine how happy we would be if we were still together. But you always cared for your happiness, not ours.

I know you regretted leaving me. And I'm so in love with you that I would run back into your arms. But no matter how much I love you, I'm not here to be someone's second option.

Don't waste your time on idiots
who couldn't love you.

Oh, I miss how your lips
tasted like cigarettes
and alcohol every night.

You easily gave up on me.
But I had myself, and that's
all I needed to save me.

I never did lose you,
for you were never mine.

How they treat you when they are angry is how they are always going to treat you.

- A kind note.

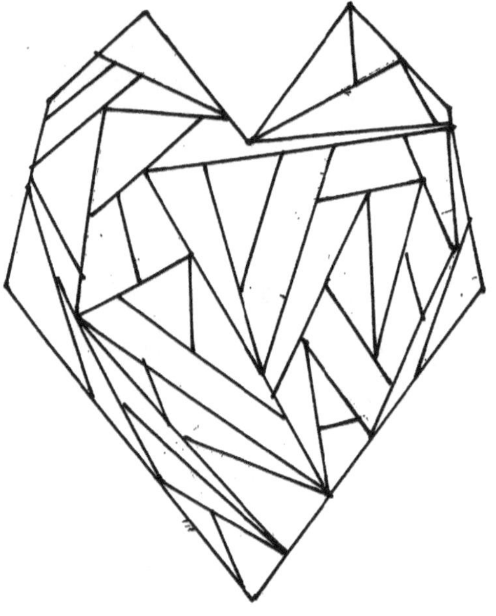

I have always walked away with a smile on my face and a broken heart.

Don't take me wrong. I might be broken, but flowers are growing from every crack you left in my chest.

So many broken hearts,
so many broken pieces,
so much of pain
turning into power.

Your love ain't true if it's here to crack
open every old wound in my heart.

Leave

And still

The flowers will bloom

The sun will shine

The stars will twinkle

For my heart

Will still be beating

With love

Inside

You are art only a true artist will appreciate.
You are love only a true lover will appreciate.
You are a soul. Only a true body will appreciate.

92

This emptiness is what i'm
going to fall in love with.

The world for me ended that night. But I woke up the next morning and started a new one.

And when you are around, my heart turns from red to pink, from pink to orange, from orange to yellow.

95

Sometimes it's love.
Sometimes it's stupidity.

- Honestly

It doesn't matter how much love this heart has for you. It doesn't matter how much I want you to stay. I know that I love you, and I always will.

- But it's time to let you go.

And if you ever think of breaking my heart. Break it with the truth and some passion in your heart.

Losing you was easier than loving you.

Loving and being loved in return is one of the best feelings, but it's rare. Being loved in return is rare compared to falling in love. Not everyone is going to love you back, but the day one does, you will know that love is the greatest thing to happen in your life.

- Love regardless.

All your heart needs is a little bit of love to bloom like an exquisite flower.

I have seen pain and happiness walk into the same room. I have seen pain ruin a heart. I have seen a broken heart famish, and I have seen the happiest people break into a million pieces.

Love is the only feeling that can make us the happiest and shatter our hearts at the same time.

Yes, it hurts. But I won't let pain take over my heart. I will let love rule it, regardless of the pain it's going through.

- I'm broken, but still beautiful.

It's okay to be lost for a while and feel the way you feel right now. Someday soon, you will come across something that's going to make you happy. And in that happiness, you will find yourself.

Don't go back to the same place,
finding for the same love you
always wanted. There was no love,
and there is still no love there.

Somedays I wish you never left, but then I
look back and see how strong it made me.
And that's how I don't miss you anymore.

My heart deserves a lover who will find beauty in between all these cracks.

Don't push away the ones who love you for someone who is just pretending to love you.

Stop fighting for a love that never wanted to stay in the first place.

Perhaps you never deserved me, nor a
generous and strong heart like mine.

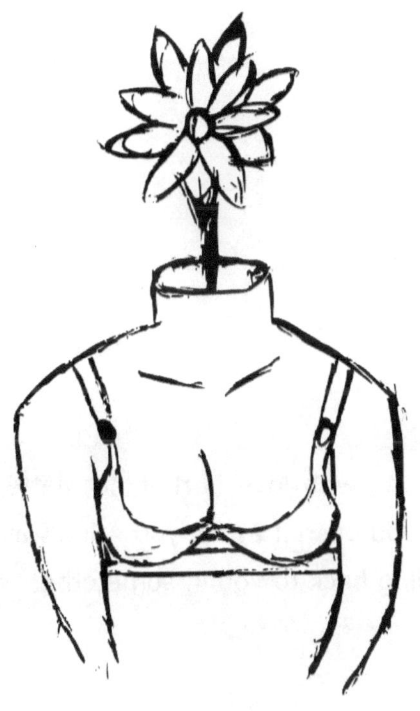

I choose the way I feel, and I will always choose happiness and myself over anything else.

The thing with love is that no matter how much you push it away, you will always find it coming back to you in some other way.

Your departure made me feel many things. It made me realize the importance of loving myself. It made me protect my heart.

I'm tired of falling for people who
treat my heart like a punching bag.

We were born in the process of making love. And lucky enough to be a part of a love that nourishes our soul.

I'm going to build a home in my heart, a home no one can vandalize.

Be gentle with my heart. It
may look strong, but it has
been through a rough trail.

The pain was my blessing in disguise. It made my heart bleed from places I thought it never would. It taught my heart to love itself with immense power. And in the end, it made my heart stronger.

This heart doesn't fall in
love anymore. It grows.

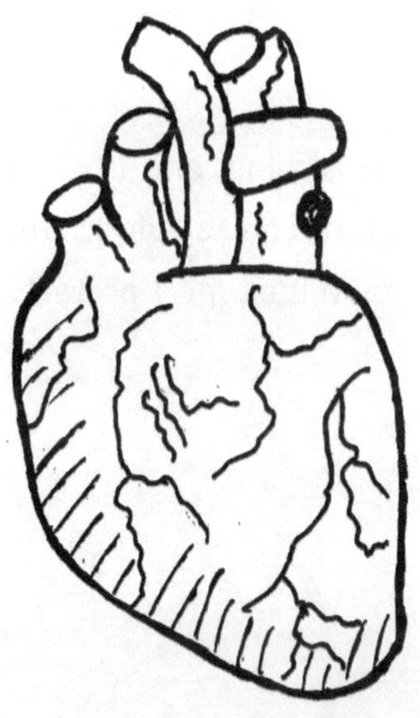

This heart is mine, and I have given it
to enough of you to ruin it. This heart
is mine, and it's time I protect it.

119

Be the reason your heart
believes in love again.

Thank you for reading

Your love and support means a lot

Instagram - @healwithhansel
Facebook - @h. d costa